You Want Me to Do What Now?

101 of the worst job titles around

SARAH JACKSON

Copyright © 2019 by Sarah Jackson & Big Bulb Books

All rights reserved. This book or any portion thereof may not be reproduced or used in any manner whatsoever without the express written permission of the publisher, except for the use of brief quotations in a book review or scholarly journal.

All images have been sourced through **https://pixabay.com**

First Printing 2019

ISBN: 978-0-9945663-5-5

Big Bulb Books

2020

DEDICATION

This book is dedicated to all of the job seekers out there. May your search be amusing and fruitful.

CONTENTS

Forward	1
Delusory Descriptions	3
Jarring Job Titles	26
Perilous Punctuation	43
Histrionic Honorifics	52
Overinflated Offerings	65
Nonsensical Names	76
Off-colour Options	99
Closing Remarks	113
Acknowledgements	*114*
Index	*115*
About the Author	*120*

"You want me to do what now?"

FORWARD

About two years ago I started looking at employment web sites, in order to secure some part-time work to supplement my writing income. As I worked my way through the various job websites, I came across a wide variety of position titles, job descriptions and advertisements. These ranged from the vague and confusing, to the downright ludicrous. Clearly, these weren't the jobs for me. But who *were* they for? And what, exactly, was a person supposed to do, when they were appointed to these positions?

It's essential that advertisers put some thought into how a job title reads, and what other, unintended meanings, could be derived from their innocently placed classifieds. For the diligent jobseeker there are more than a few laughs to be had.

This book provides you with 101 of my favourite job titles. All are recorded exactly as they were listed on the website/advertising source (business names have been removed to protect the guilty).

The position titles are sorted into seven broad categories, each with a specific (and peculiar) feature. Many of the jobs could easily fit into more than one of the categories, but I have selected the one that best describes it.

I'm certain that you'll be able to see yourself with some of these titles on your business card. Happy job hunting.

DELUSORY DESCRIPTIONS

Have you ever come across a position title that whets your appetite with promises of an interesting and exciting career, only to discover that it was all a bit misleading?

The first set of our 101 job titles all fit into the "bit of a lie" category:

1. Food and Beverage Lover

This job certainly has promise. Who doesn't love food and beverages? I wonder what joys await the lovers of food and beverages who apply for this position.

The role the employer was actually advertising:

Food lovers indeed. A closer examination of the role did not reveal anything to suggest that consuming or enjoying products was part of the job. The advertisement was for a restaurant chain (think low-rent/poor quality) looking for wait staff.

2. Vintage Retail Assistant

VINTAGE RETAIL ASSISTANT

It's good to see that employers are advertising positions specifically for the over-50s.

The role the employer was actually advertising:

A shop selling vintage clothing was looking for a part-time sales assistant. The age of the assistant was not a factor.

3. Complaints and Disputes Officer

I would be very happy to offer my services to your organisation. I pledge to complain bitterly at every opportunity and instigate as many disputes as required. I suspect that there would be some stiff competition for this role.

The role the employer was actually advertising:

A government agency was looking for an administrative clerk to compile and maintain a register of complaints. It's worth noting that many 'governments' bodies advertise jobs with crazy position titles and have position descriptions full of weasel words. Study the advertisement carefully before applying.

4. Bell Attendant

Do you have experience with bells? Are you prepared to attend to them, and cater to their every need? This could be the role for you.

The role the employer was actually advertising:

No, you aren't expected to look after bells in this job. 'Bell attendant' appears to be a modern, and perhaps nicer way of describing a 'bellhop'. Expect to be carrying bags for hotel customers if you take on this role.

5. University Dockhands

I know that some universities have docks for their rowing and boating clubs, and others have docks for ferry services. But I'm not aware of any universities that have a dock so sizeable that it requires a dockhand, casual or otherwise.

The role the employer was actually advertising:

This employer was a shipping company looking for part-time/casual staff to work over the university holidays.

"You want me to do what now?"

6. *Points Person*

Are you good at pointing? Or, do you know a lot of points (on any topic)? Perhaps you have a lot of points (Could be driver's licence, fly-buys, grocery store program maybe)? Yes? This could be the job for you.

The role the employer was actually advertising:

This role was being advertised by a city council, and was, surprisingly, for a person to work at a garbage tip (dump). It was either for a person to work at a particular transfer point (say the recycling station) or to direct (point) people to the correct place to dump their rubbish.

7. *Long Life Assistant*

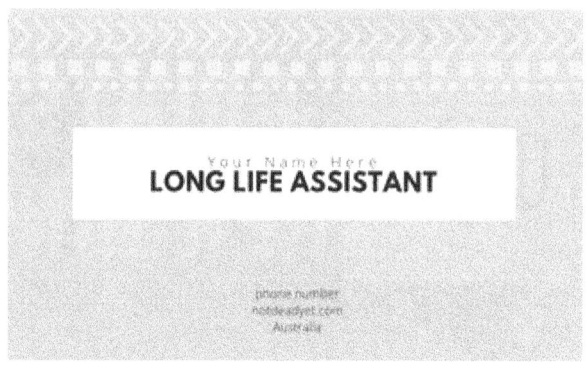

This employer is tired of assistants who go off and die after a couple of days? Are you likely to be around for the long haul? Are you in reasonable health? This could be the job for you.

The role the employer was actually advertising:

A small grocery retailer placed this advertisement. The position title was meant to describe a shelf stacker/night-fill person who looks after stock rotation. But I'm sure not dying the second you start the job would also be advantageous.

"You want me to do what now?"

8. Banquet Attendant

Sounds delightful. What a wonderful occupation. I'll start with champagne cocktail and a couple of canapés. No? What else could they possibly mean by 'banquet attendant'?

The role the employer was actually advertising:

Sadly, you haven't been invited to get paid to attend a function. A large hotel was looking for catering staff to wait tables at functions.

9. Vacation Student

Are you looking to continue your studies? I'm keen on this field of study, and it being a paid role just adds to the appeal. Sign me up.

The role the employer was actually advertising:

A logistics company was advertising for juniors to work in their distribution centre over the school and university holidays.

10. Food and Beverage Attendant

Do you have experience attending to the needs of food and/or beverages? I don't know about you, but if anyone's going to attend to my food and beverages it will be me. (Not that my food or beverages are particularly demanding of my time and resources).

The role the employer was actually advertising:

In the same vein as the "Food and Beverage Lover" and "Banquet Attendant". A café/restaurant was looking for wait staff. Both food and bar service.

11. Pie Dealer

Is this kind of like a drug dealer? I suspect yes, but it's safer, lower paid and working with a product more people are interested in.

The role the employer was actually advertising:

A fast food chain was looking for a sales assistant for one of their stores. Go on, guess what they sell.

12. Gym Attendant

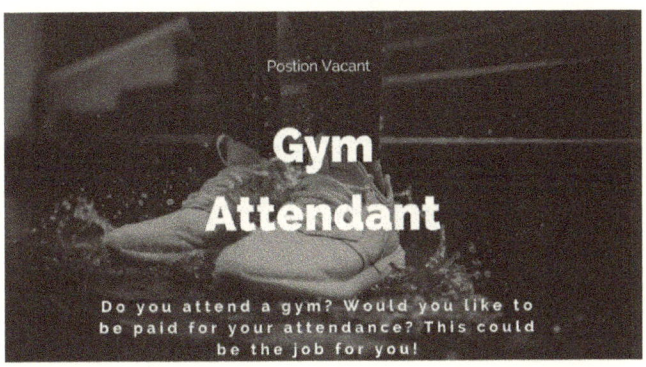

Would you like to be paid to attend the gym? What kind of experience do you have attending gyms? This is an ideal job for a fitness fanatic who can't afford the gym fees. Or maybe for a person who needs extra motivation to go!

The role the employer was actually advertising:

This employer was advertising for a bit of everything. They were looking for someone who could operate as a trainer, look after equipment, site maintenance and to sell memberships (I'd be interested to see how much of the role was centered around the sales part of the job).

13. Truck Jockey

And they're off and racing! Are you keen to join the competitive world of truck racing? Are you interested in becoming a jockey but just aren't that into horses? Or maintaining a very low body mass for that matter? This could be the job for you?

The role the employer was actually advertising:

A transport company was looking for staff to travel with licensed truck drivers to read maps, complete paperwork and lift things.

14. Opening Wine Team

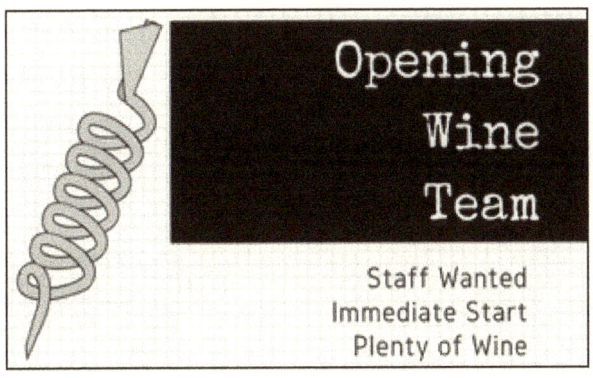

Are you keen to work for a company that has such a large volume of wine that it requires an entire team to open it? I would be happy to open the wine, if I was then able to sample it.

The role the employer was actually advertising:

I am uncertain if this position was for a chef, kitchen hand, bar staff or a sommelier (wine steward). The advertisement blathered on incoherently about chefs and food. The word 'wine' in the title leads me to believe that this was advertising for bar staff.

"You want me to do what now?"

15. Party Enthusiast

I like parties, and it's fair to say that I'm enthusiastic about them. This sounds like a job for me. When I looked closer, the job didn't seem to involve attending any parties, events or functions. It wasn't for an events planner, or even a party clown.

The role the employer was actually advertising:

The advertisement was for a retail sales assistant in a party-supply section of a store – all blowing up balloons and dealing with pushy parents and naughty kids.

16. Crew

Ahoy matey! Looking for an exciting life at sea? Crew members wanted.

The role the employer was actually advertising:

No, this job advertisement wasn't for pirates, sailors, or even flight attendants. Believe it or not, this is a job for a fast-food worker. This one is all about operating the cash register, customer service, clearing tables and flipping burgers.

17. Experienced Wine Bar Attendant

Pick Me! This sounds like my sort of job. I have had an abundance of experience attending wine bars. And not just wine bars. My extensive experience includes pubs, hotels, restaurants, cocktail lounges and nightclubs.

The role the employer was actually advertising:

A 'trendy' venue was looking for bar staff.

18. Retail Artist

Are you a painter or sculptor looking to provide art for retailers? If so, then this is not the role for you.

The role the employer was actually advertising:

This retail artist job referred to a position as a sales clerk on a make-up/cosmetics counter in a shop. Could be worse, it could be advertising for someone to make sandwiches and coffees.

19. Merchandise Compliance Officer

Nobody likes difficult, ill-mannered or non-compliant merchandise.

The role the employer was actually advertising:

I couldn't really make out what this role entails. Keeping shelves tidy perhaps? Patrolling the aisles? The employer (and industry) was not clearly stated. This role could be for what is often referred to as a 'Loss Prevention Officer" (to stop folk from nicking stuff), or some sort of logistics officer (to check on stock levels). It may be for a person to check newly manufactured merchandise, to ensure that it meets quality assurance requirements.

20. *Vintage Cellar Hand*

Older person required to work in a cellar. Isn't it wonderful to see employers embracing mature-aged workers – even if they are putting them in a basement.

The role the employer was actually advertising:

The employer was a winery, which was looking for a specialist in vintage wines to assist with their cellar door (shop) operations. Would it have really been that difficult to change the advertisement to read "Assistant required for a vintage wine cellar"? Or even a simple "Winery Operations Assistant."

21. Ground Handler

Is this something like a dog handler? Are you a person who can get 'ground' into line? Perhaps it's a role for some sort of mystic, who gets psychic readings from the soil? Maybe the employer is after a horticulturalist, or environmental scientist who tests soils?

The role the employer was actually advertising:

This advertisement was for a small airline looking for a person to work on their counter in the airport terminal.

22. *Floor Supervisor*

Nobody likes an unruly floor. Do you have experience supervising a variety of flooring to ensure that it does its job – stopping things from falling into the foundations, supporting furniture, etc.

The role the employer was actually advertising:

This employer was a medium-sized industrial company. The position was for a person to supervise staff on a factory floor.

JARRING JOB TITLES

Our second set of job titles includes the ones that sound peculiar, generate more questions than answers, and generally cause one to raise an inquisitive eyebrow. These are job titles that make you go "hmm".

We start with job entry number 23.

23. Sales Hunter

Do you have visions of yourself trekking through a distant jungle in search of prey? Yes? Well, you'll get none of that here.

The role the employer was actually advertising:

There was limited information on the employer, the role, or the working conditions. Always a bad sign. Sadly, this advertisement wasn't for an exciting adventure. It was more likely for a dodgy, commission-only, door-to-door salesperson, cold-caller, or telemarketing operator.

24. Client Success Specialists

When I read job titles like this, I automatically wonder if the opposite exists. Is there a 'Client Failure Specialist' out there somewhere? What sort of a role does a 'Client Success Specialist' have anyway? And who are their clients? Is this some sort of business support role? Coaching? Training?

The role the employer was actually advertising:

This position was all about sales; specifically selling a software package to unsuspecting businesses. Cold calling and commission only.

25. Inbound Consumer Sales

Do you have experience selling inbound consumers? How about outbound consumers? What's an 'inbound consumer' anyway? And why would anyone want to buy one?

The role the employer was actually advertising:

This convoluted title was for a call centre worker. I guess that 'inbound' could mean anything from dealing with casual inquiries, to processing sales, or handling complaints.

26. Café All Rounder Lady

Lady? Really? I don't know that many of us actually have a formal title. Perhaps they are referring to a person who is lady-like? I'm not quite sure what an 'all rounder lady' is either.

The role the employer was actually advertising:

An old-fashioned, hospitality employer was looking for a female staff member to serve customers, prepare food, wash up and operate the till. (And possibly be sexually harassed.)

27. Continuous Improvement Coordinator

Are you an experienced continuous improvement coordinator? What activity was in such an appalling state that it required continuous improvement? And how does one coordinate it?

The role the employer was actually advertising:

A government department advertised the position, so it could be for anything. A thorough review of the position description gave a few clues. The job activities appear to involve bullying and intimidating staff. Great role for some.

28. Practice Advice Coach

I wasn't sure if this role was for a person who was practicing to be an 'advice coach', or whether it was for a 'coach' who gives 'practice advice' (as in football practice). It may also be for a person to provide advice to people running a 'practice' (for example a medical practice).

The role the employer was actually advertising:

The employer was a 'wealth management' firm (one of my favourite types of dodgy businesses/employers). The role seemed to involve training/coaching staff in ways to relieve the client base of their hard-earned cash.

29. Integration Assistant

There's something very creepy about this style of job title. It reminds me of '1984', forced assimilation and other fascist ruling styles. I wonder what, or who, requires integration?

The role the employer was actually advertising:

Surprisingly, this position was advertised by a media publisher (magazines). The role seemed to be for an administration assistant with some experience in communications. The position description was extensive, but it still didn't make clear what was being integrated. Confusing and strange.

30. Lead Generation

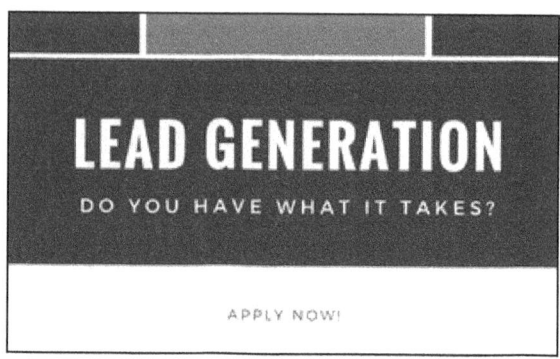

Do you have what it takes to be a 'Lead Generation'? Or lead a generation? Can you be a 'generation'? I know that you can be part of a generation.

The role the employer was actually advertising:

This advertisement was for a call centre telemarketing role. These positions are frequently advertised as 'no selling, only lead generation'. You will still be making cold calls and annoying people. Instead of making the sales yourself you're going to be convincing people to let the company representative either come to their door or hound them continuously over the phone. Fun times.

31. Customer Service Gun

I understand the 'Customer Service' element, but what is a 'Gun'? One recalls the expression 'under the gun' (originally an old shearing term). It could mean either a military situation where you are physically under artillery, or it can mean being under pressure. Neither is appealing.

The role the employer was actually advertising:

Closer inspection of the advertisement indicated that it was for a retail sales assistant position. The catch - the successful candidate would also do office work, bookkeeping, logistics and sales. With no advertised salary, one suspects that it is the 'under pressure' part of 'Gun'.

"You want me to do what now?"

32. Truck and Dog Driver

I get the truck driver part, but what is a dog driver? I know that you can 'drive' a dog sled team. But I wouldn't have thought that there was much call for that in this neck of the woods. Would you be expected to drive both at one?

The role the employer was actually advertising:

This title strikes alarm in the heart of non-transport industry people. No, there aren't any dogs in peril. A 'dog' refers to both a trailer that is attached to a main/lead trailer, and a device used to tension chains to secure the load.

33. Allocations Analyst

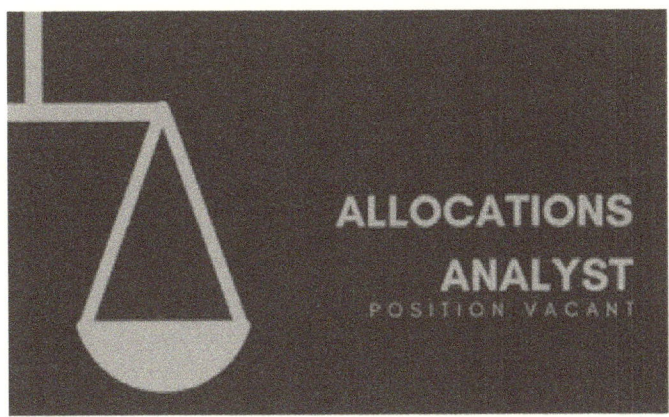

What on earth is an "Allocations Analyst"? Is this person involved in finance? Or project management? Or maybe a little of both. It certainly sounds like some sort of an office job.

The role the employer was actually advertising:

This rather important-sounding role turned out to be a stock control (store person) position – as in stacking shelves, counting inventory and placing orders.

34. Quality Support Advisor

Are you 'quality'? Are you a 'support advisor'? I wonder how this role compares to a support advisor lacking in quality? I wonder what type of advisor the role supports?

The role the employer was actually advertising:

The position description provided very little information about the employer and the nature of the business. I suspect that the job was advertising for a Human Resources role but can't be certain.

35. Remote Phone Sales Executive

Are you a person who doesn't easily engage with others? A bit shy perhaps? Or maybe someone who isn't really interested in their work? A job as a Remote Phone Sales Executive may be for you. Perhaps the 'Sales Executive' part isn't what 'remote' refers to? When I buy a phone, I actually want it with me and not somewhere 'remote'.

The role the employer was actually advertising:

A call centre (the remote part) was looking for telemarketers to flog off mobile phones. Doesn't the 'executive' bit make you chuckle?

36. Merchandiser Sales Support

Well. This is a very confusing job title. I'm not sure if you are required to support the sale of merchandisers, or support merchandisers with sales.

The role the employer was actually advertising:

I originally thought that this was for a sales assistant position, but on closer inspection it looked more like a cleaner/shelf stacker/stock control role, with a little bit of underpaid work as a Window Dresser/Display person on the side.

37. Domestic Violence Advocate

> **Domestic Violence Advocate!**
>
> Are you an advocate of domestic violence? If so, there's a job to suit you.

Do you support domestic violence? Would you like to advocate for it? A jarring job title indeed!

The role the employer was actually advertising:

I am certain that this position title describes a support role for victims, rather than that of a role promoting and supporting domestic violence. But then again, it's a strange world.

38. Insight Analyst

Oh, my! What on earth is an 'Insight Analyst'? 'Insight' into what exactly? And how does one analyse insights. Imagine explaining this one to your Grandmother.

The role the employer was actually advertising:

A mysterious job title for someone whose role is strictly marketing and sales. No details on the employer, wages or conditions.

PERILOUS PUNCTUATION

As a writer, I'm very aware of the importance of punctuation. The order of words, absence of a comma, or even a missing dash, can create unintended, and sometimes amusing, meanings.

Advertisers, please be sure to spend the money to ensure that those all-important extra words and symbols are included in your text.

Our next set of job titles can be read a number of ways:

39. Meat Team Member

Are you made of meat? Not sure if I qualify here. Humans are technically mostly water, but I guess it would be reasonable to say that we're made of meat.

The role the employer was actually advertising:

A large supermarket chain was looking for someone (not necessarily trade qualified or made of meat) to work in the butchery section of the store.

40. Casual Refugee Youth Worker

Are you a 'Refugee' and a 'Youth Worker'? And are you 'Casual'. Maybe 'casual' isn't such a big deal, and if you're a little 'formal' they'll employ you anyway?

The role the employer was actually advertising:

A community organisation was looking for a welfare worker to assist with recently arrived, young refugees.

41. Principal Consultant Rail

I wasn't aware that a rail was able to apply for jobs. I also had no idea that there were different job levels available for rails.

The role the employer was actually advertising:

This government position was for a project manager to work in the transport (railways) industry. A dash between 'Consultant' and 'Rail' would have made all the difference.

"You want me to do what now?"

42. Farm Hand Horses

It would take a very clever horse indeed to work as a farm hand. Most horses gallop about paddocks, whiney occasionally and eat a lot of hay.

The role the employer was actually advertising:

I suspect that this advertisement needed a dash between 'Farm Hand' and 'Horses'. The role was for a farm hand on a horse stud. But I'm sure that they'd be happy to consider horses too.

43. Casual Nanny

Hmm, no thanks. If I need the services of a Nanny, I want he/she to be alert and on-the-job for the duration of their shift. Perhaps this should read "Nanny – Casual hours"

The role the employer was actually advertising:

There was almost no information on the employer, or details of the job. I couldn't even see how many children the 'Casual Nanny' was expected to look after or work out the shift details. I suspect that this advertisement is looking for an individual to be available for on-call babysitting.

44. Entry Level Finance

I'm not entirely sure what a 'Finance' is, but I know that it's not me - entry level or otherwise. I suspect that this should read "Finance – Entry Level position".

The role the employer was actually advertising:

The employer was advertising for an 'office all-rounder' to perform bookkeeping, customer service and general administration duties. I guess that 'entry level' means that you make the tea and coffee.

45. Collections Customer Service

I wonder what a 'Collections Customer' is? I imagine that the service they require depends on the sort of things that the customer is collecting. Perhaps this is another warehouse/logistics roles?

The role the employer was actually advertising:

This delightful job title sounds pleasant enough but is actually for a call centre debt collector. Not sure how the customers feel about this service.

46. Kitchen Hand/Food Truck

I would consider the kitchen hand role, but don't think that I have what it takes to make the registration requirements to become a food truck.

The role the employer was actually advertising:

Would it have been so difficult for the advertiser to add 'for a' between 'hand' and 'food"? I guess that we should be grateful that they paid to have a "/" between the words.

HISTRIONIC HONOURIFICS

I am always amused by this particular set of job titles. To me these overinflated, over-enthusiastic job titles seem to automatically mean that the job advertised has either poor wages and condition and/or involves boring and difficult work.

See what you think of this selection of exciting and power-packed position titles. I'm sure that you'd be proud to have any of these on your business card.

"You want me to do what now?"

47. Superheroes!

Are you Batman? Wonder Woman? The Flash? Maybe you're a lesser-known superhero? Either way, there's a company out there looking for you.

The role the employer was actually advertising:

This was another one of those dodgy-looking advertisements placed by an unknown company. The position description was full of buzzwords and catch phrases. On closer inspection it appeared to be some sort of web design role but was more likely to involve working in an IT call centre.

48. Audience Insights Officer

Do you know much about audiences? Would you say that you have insight into them? I'm not exactly certain what 'insight' refers to. Perhaps this role is for a stage psychic or a magician.

The role the employer was actually advertising:

The position was advertised by a museum. The selection criteria emphasised the need for excellent communication skills, but there was a large emphasis on sales. I couldn't work out if this was a membership sales or retail shop role. Perhaps it's for something entirely different.

49. Lively Animated Manager

I guess I'd rather employ one of these than a lifeless, stagnant manager.

The role the employer was actually advertising:

I couldn't make out what industry the employer was in but judging from the use of buzz words and catch phrases, I imagine that the job was in a call centre or sales environment.

50. Talent Acquisition Specialist

Now, I bet that you're expecting this advertisement to be for some sort of talent scout for a theatre, film company or even a music-related business? No? Maybe it's for some recruitment-style Human Resources position?

The role the employer was actually advertising:

This was an advertisement for a business loans officer in a bank. Go figure?

51. Mission Control Centre Engagement

"Ground Control to Major Tom". If you are looking for a groovy job with a space agency, then this is not the one for you.

The role the employer was actually advertising:

The employer was a 'modern' information technology services provider. I would be conducting a careful check of this company's background and business credentials before submitting an application. Hokey advertising ploys to attract staff do not bode well for future success. This role was for an IT call centre/help desk person. Disappointing!

52. Family Strengthening Officer

Fitness Instructor required to set up weight training programs for families. No? Perhaps they were advertising for a person to help with both diet, and exercise programs?

The role the employer was actually advertising:

A community agency, specialising in early childhood development, was looking for a qualified person to assist people with limited parenting skills. The position descriptions placed a lot of emphasis on 'risk factors' and 'protective issues'. Tough gig.

53. Home Onboarding Pro

Not quite sure what 'home onboarding' is, or what it takes to be considered a 'pro'. Perhaps this employer is looking for a person with a lot of experience as a lodger.

The role the employer was actually advertising:

Although the job advertisement was scant on detail, it would appear that the mystery employer was looking for what used to be known as a Property Manager – specifically, one to look after Airbnb style residences.

54. Sourcing Execution Specialist

I wasn't certain if this advertisement was for a company looking for (as in they were sourcing) an execution specialist, or whether they were after a person who could employ (source) execution specialists. Either way, it's a great position for someone with an interest in capital punishment.

The role the employer was actually advertising:

A Human Resources company was advertising the position. The position description was full of weasel words. I'm not sure what the role entailed, or how executions came into it.

55. Computer Trainer

Kind of like a dog trainer, except with computers. Must be able to get them to 'sit', 'beg' and 'roll-over' on command.

The role the employer was actually advertising:

A training provider was looking for a qualified and experienced trainer to provide classes for people (yes, people), to teach them how to use a variety of computer programs.

56. Loyalty Campaign Specialist

Person required to convince/coerce people to be loyal. Sounds like a political position in a fascist dictatorship.

The role the employer was actually advertising:

A person was required to undertake promotions and marketing for a store's loyalty card program. This position, advertised by a retail fashion chain, included many duties requiring the incumbent to 'execute campaigns' and develop 'brand loyalty' (perhaps they should consider supplying an excellent product for starters). There were 13 selection criteria, each being a variation on the two previously mentioned tasks. Brevity was not a requirement.

57. Bequest Relationship Coordinator

Hmm. This rather fancy title gives away the purpose of the role with word "bequest".

The role the employer was actually advertising:

You will be badgering people into leaving charitable donations as part of their Last Will and Testament. If you're *really* lucky it will be a job in a call centre.

58. Manager Positive Behaviour Support

I'm rather keen on the Negative Behaviour Support role myself. A very confusing job title indeed. How does one support positive behaviour? The title suggests a "Manager". Is the role managing those who deliver the positive behaviour support?

The role the employer was actually advertising:

This employer, a disability support services organisation, was looking for an experienced person to work with 'high-needs' clients. A difficult, challenging and most likely, underpaid position.

OVERINFLATED OFFERINGS

These job titles, like their 'histrionic' cousins, suggest roles that are far above the actual station of the position. I guess that the purpose of the exaggerated titles is to encourage applicants to believe that the positions aren't the base grade jobs that they are (as reflected in the advertised duties and salaries).

This style of advertising merely serves to confuse the job seeker, and suitable candidates may pass over the advertisement not realising what the job actually is.

Here are a number of examples of 'overinflated offerings'. There could be a job for you in this fascinating set of occupations.

59. First Impressions Manager

What a wonderful example to start off this section of the book. First impressions indeed. What does a "First Impressions Manager" actually do?

The role the employer was actually advertising:

The employer was a groovy-funky Human Resources Management company. And the "First Impressions Manager"? This was an advertisement for a receptionist. Really, a receptionist! A person to sit on the front desk, answer phones, take messages, manage diaries (there's the management part of the role), type, greet people and make cups of tea and coffee. Junior salary only, for this high-level position.

60. Brand Ambassador

Wow! A position for an ambassador is being advertised on-line. This could be a glamourous job? I wonder what opportunities and interesting experiences are offered in this role?

The role the employer was actually advertising:

Sounds important? Well, it isn't. Welcome to the world of the retail salesclerk. This type of job is usually advertised by clothing retail chains.

61. Replenishment Officer

Sounds rather dramatic, doesn't it? What or who requires replenishment? And why does it require an 'officer'. Is it an office job? A job for military personnel perhaps? It may even be a role for a tea lady/gentleman?

The role the employer was actually advertising:

You guessed it. This was another over-inflated job title describing a shelf-stacker/night-fill person for a supermarket.

"You want me to do what now?"

62. Third in Charge

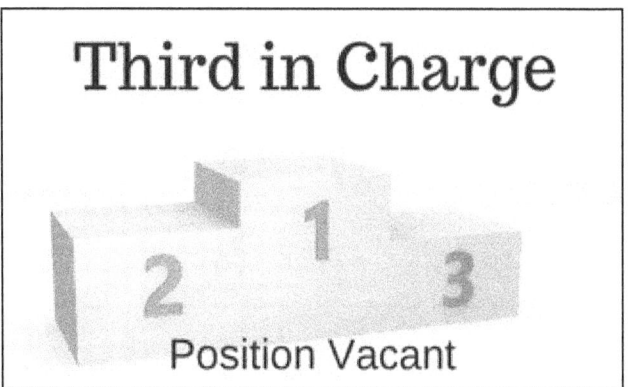

Oh, the prestigious. What a coveted role this must be. I can just imagine the high-level meetings, perks and executive salary that this fashion chain-store would be offering the successful candidate.

The role the employer was actually advertising:

Not the First in Charge. Not even the Second in Charge. Sounds like this role is for a general dogs body (lackey) with high levels of responsibility and low wages. If anything goes wrong, expect the Third in Charge to carry the can.

63. Appointment Setter

This sounds like a position for a person to manage diaries, set up meetings, and maybe book travel.

The role the employer was actually advertising:

Don't be fooled into thinking that this is some sort of receptionist position. The advertisement gave away very little information on the employer and the nature of the role. This was most likely advertising a door-to-door sales or cold-call/telemarketing operation. Expect to be hounding people into making appointments to allow high-pressure salespeople into their homes. Likely to be a low retainer and/or commission only work.

64. Style Consultant

Does this position sound appealing? Are you looking for work as a fashion designer? Maybe an interior designer? Fashion buyer? Perhaps a high-level consultant? Yes? Then you need to keep looking.

The role the employer was actually advertising:

This position was for a retail clerk for a women's dress store (and not a high-end one either. Think 'mature shopper').

"You want me to do what now?"

65. Guest Services Agent

Is this kind of like a secret agent? I wonder what type of services this agent will be sourcing (or providing)?

The role the employer was actually advertising:

The employer was a medium-sized hotel chain. The position looked like it was for a Concierge, but on further inspection the role turned out to be a desk clerk. A very busy desk clerk (assuming that the hotel had moderate patronage).

66. Fill Associates

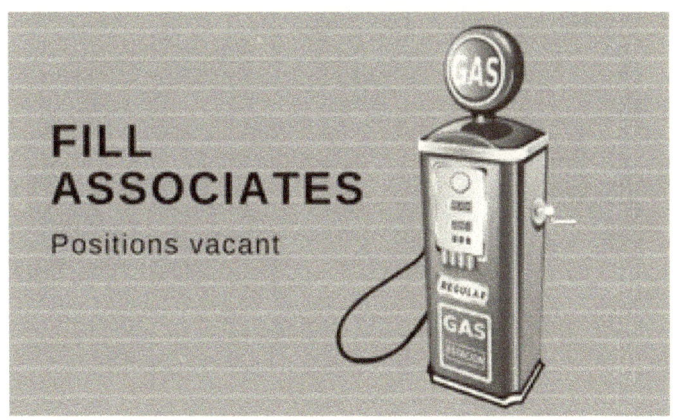

'Fill Associate'? Does this refer to 'fill' in the landscaping and construction sense? Perhaps it's for a service station attendant? And an 'Associate'? Is the position for a senior/high ranking member of the company? I doubt it.

The role the employer was actually advertising:

This job advertisement was a rather vague way of describing the not-very-prestigious role of shelf-stacker, or 'night-fill' staff member for a supermarket.

67. Management Support Officer Lead Job

Position available for anyone who can work out what the job is.

If it weren't for the inclusion of the word 'job' at the end of the position title, this role would sound rather important. What is 'Management Support'? Is this office administration? A 'Personal Assistant' role? And why is it the 'Lead Job'? Is it for a head of the typing pool? That's a genuinely important role.

The role the employer was actually advertising:

I couldn't really tell what type of position was being advertised. The employer was a telemarketing sales company, so one could assume that the job was for a cold call salesperson, or maybe a PA to the manager, or maybe a bit of both.

68. Capability Lead

What exactly does a 'Capability Lead' do? What is meant by 'Capability' and why does it require leading? A bizarre string of weasel words!

The role the employer was actually advertising:

I couldn't work out what this job title was actually describing. The position description mentioned that a qualification in Human Resource Management was required. Hopefully, it was for a person to re-work the company's job titles and position description.

NONSENSICAL NAMES

This next set of job titles feature those that either make no sense at all or are generally uninformative. Either way, they don't seem to describe anything much in particular.

"You want me to do what now?"

69. Product Owner/Analyst

Is this a position for a person who reviews the quality and standard of products? I own a lot of products. And I have worked as an analyst. Maybe this is the job I'm looking for?

The role the employer was actually advertising:

Even after reading the position description three times, I was still unable to work out what types of tasks were involved. I suspect that the advertisement was for some type of commission-only sales role, or pyramid scheme operation. Lots of weasel words, little information.

70. People Services Consultant

People Services Consultant

POSITION VACANT

So, what are 'People Services' exactly? And why do others need to be consulted on them. Are we talking health and medical services? Beautician's services, wait staff?

The role the employer was actually advertising:

This position was for a government department. The advertisement was so full of catch phrases and weasel words that it was difficult to work out what the job entailed. It was most likely a position for a Human Resources staff member with expertise in workforce planning. But it could have just as easily have been for a bathroom attendant.

71. Casual Keyholder Sales Assistant

> **Position Vacant**
>
> Casual Keyholder Sales Assistant

Are you an experienced 'keyholder salesperson'? What is a 'keyholder salesperson'? What is a 'keyholder'? And why is it presented as a single word instead of two?

The role the employer was actually advertising:

The advertisement appeared to be for a retail sales assistant. But not just a sales assistant – this one had a hand in budget planning, stock processing and merchandising. There was no explanation of what the 'keyholder' part referred to.

72. Therapeutic Residential Care Stand Up Staff

Well, we wouldn't want our Therapeutic Residential Care staff to be sitting down, now would we? Could they be looking for a 'stand-up' guy or gal? Is this some sort of comedy act? Perhaps it's part of an alternative therapies treatment program?

The role the employer was actually advertising:

The position was being advertised by an aged care facility, but the exact nature of the role wasn't clear. Perhaps it was for an Occupational Therapist or Physiotherapist to assist people with mobility issues.

73. Direct Services Coordinator

DIRECT SERVICES COORDINATOR

If you know what this job does, then maybe you'd like to apply for the vacant position

This is a bizarre job title in that there is no indication of what services (direct or otherwise) require coordination. Perhaps it is some sort of sales role?

The role the employer was actually advertising:

A review of the position description indicated that the employer was a community organisation. They were looking for a person to be a head social worker (preferably qualified) who was prepared to work for a less than acceptable salary.

74. Part Time People

Who or what is a part time person? And what are they when they're not people? Most of us are people all of the time. Are there people out there who can morph into other things?

The role the employer was actually advertising:

The employer was a chain of retail stores, and they were actually looking for salespeople to work part-time over the Christmas and New Year period.

"You want me to do what now?"

75. Car Groomer

Are you good with cars? How about grooming? Are you experienced in shampooing, trimming nails, cutting hair? Do you have experience in this field?

The role the employer was actually advertising:

No, this wasn't a misspelling of "Cat". The position was advertised by a car yard. I believe that these positions used to be referred to as "car washers/cleaners" or car-wash operators.

76. Gym Floor/Receptionist

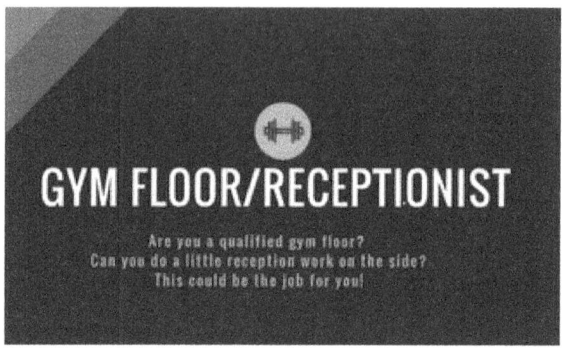

Are you a dynamic and skilled receptionist? Are you prepared to allow people to exercise, conduct classes and store gym equipment on you? Yes? Then maybe this role as a Gym Floor/Receptionist is for you. I have no issue with the receptionist part of the role, I'm just not so sure that I want to be used as a gym mat.

The role the employer was actually advertising:

The employer was a large hotel chain, and the position was for a receptionist for one of the hotel's gym facilities. The reception work was standard fare, but no explanation was provided as to how the successful candidate was to function as a gym floor.

77. Weekend Needed

I'm sure it is, but what type of job are you advertising? Are you advertising a job at all? And is it indeed on the weekend.

The role the employer was actually advertising:

There was very little information in the job advertisement to indicate what this role entailed. I have to assume that the person was required for weekend work. But doing what, exactly was a bit of a mystery.

78. Grocery Stores

Wanted, Grocery Stores. Are you a store, shop, or retail establishment? More specifically, are you a grocery store? Are you more than one?

The role the employer was actually advertising:

This chain of grocery stores (yes, that's right, the 'grocery stores' referred to the business of the employer) was looking for a number of casual retail staff to work across a number of their stores.

79. Vegetation Liaison Officer

Although I've been known to talk to my plants from time-to-time, I've never considered this to be an occupation. I wasn't even aware that vegetation needed to be liaised with. I wonder what the topics of discussion might be.

The role the employer was actually advertising:

A government agency was advertising for an experienced Environmental Officer to conduct parks and wildlife-related project work.

80. Spare Van Driver

Are you prepared to drive the spare van? Do you have experience driving spare vans? If so, then feel free to apply for this position.

The role the employer was actually advertising:

This company was looking for a casual delivery driver – person being 'spare', not the van.

"You want me to do what now?"

81. *American Restaurant/Italian Restaurant*

Are you an American restaurant? Perhaps you're an Italian restaurant? If so, then you're wanted. I certainly don't qualify for this position. I am neither an American (or Italian), nor a restaurant.

The role the employer was actually advertising:

These were two separate advertisements, appearing a couple of months apart, but the theme was the same.

Although it was clear that the business was an

'American Restaurant' (sells corn dogs, burgers, fries and pie, I guess) and an 'Italian Restaurant', it wasn't clear whether they were advertising for kitchen staff or wait staff.

Perhaps it's fashionable to advertise the nature of the business rather than the actual job being advertised.

82. Help Wanted

There can be up to ten of these positions advertised on any given day. What sort of help is wanted? Are they sick? Is a building on fire? Are they being attacked?

The role the employer was actually advertising:

This particular advertisement gave no specifics about what industry the employer belonged to. It looked like an advertisement for a sales position but could just have easily been for a person in need of CPR. You really need to check the employer and sometimes go into the job description to see what the role is. What is guaranteed is a low salary.

83. The Key Worker

Are you looking for a job as a locksmith? Or a security guard? Janitor? Receptionist at a hotel perhaps? Not sure if this is what a 'Key Worker' is? Maybe 'key' refers to 'the most important person' in the business?

The role the employer was actually advertising:

The position description advised that 'The Key Worker' was a person who supports families who are at risk of 'housing distress'. I take 'housing distress' to mean 'without one'. It appears that the employer is advertising for some sort of social or welfare worker, but they could be after a person who hands out keys to emergency accommodation.

84. Part Time Essendon

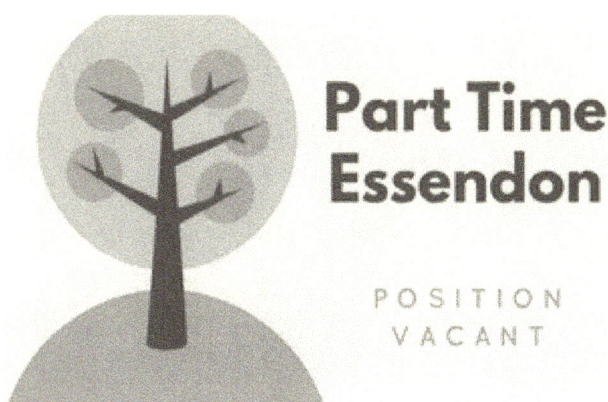

It's lovely that the suburb of Essendon has become so busy that it requires a break. And a break so lengthy that it warrants employing someone to take on the role, on a part-time basis. Not sure that I know how to be a suburb/location.

The role the employer was actually advertising:

Part time logistics staff where required to work for an employer in Essendon.

85. Assistant Controlled Entity Accountant

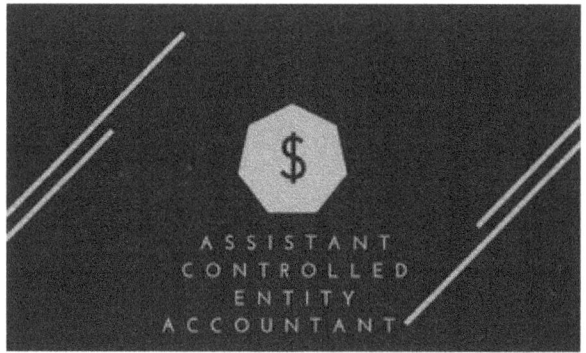

I'm not sure what an 'Assistant Controlled Entity' is, but I do know what an accountant does. I wonder if it is supposed to read 'Assistant Accountant – Controlled Entity'.

The role the employer was actually advertising:

The position appeared to be advertising for a qualified accountant with experience in budgets, annual reports and financial services generally. I couldn't find any explanation of what a 'Controlled Entity' or 'Assistant Controlled Entity' is. Perhaps this makes sense to bookkeepers and accountants.

86. Winter is Coming

I do love it when people think that it's clever to use a catch phrase or cultural reference in their job advertisements. That'll distract prospective candidates from crappy roles and sub-par wages and conditions. As for this advertisement, I was very much under the impression that "winter was here". At least it had arrived from my last viewing of the show this refers to.

The role the employer was actually advertising:

There was no clear indication of who the employer was. I'm not sure how much a role as 'Winter is coming' pays, but the job seems to involve waiting on tables.

87. Weed Programs Facilitator

Potheads across the city were getting excited about this one. I wonder what type of 'Weed Programs' were being facilitated.

The role the employer was actually advertising:

Not as exciting as it sounds. A local council was advertising for a gardener/horticulturalist to set up a community awareness program to identify and manage noxious weeds (as in unwanted plants, not illegal drugs)

88. The Enabling Capability Platform

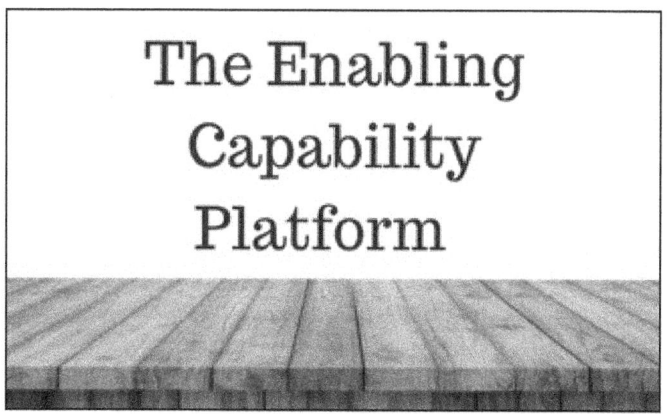

Bizarre advertisement from an employer looking to take on a new staff member to be a 'platform'. And the 'enabling capability' platform at that. Could this be advertising for a developer of some sort of IT platform? Maybe it's a construction platform (scaffolding) or perhaps an oilrig/drilling platform?

The role the employer was actually advertising:

I can't say with any certainty what role this employer was advertising. I can't even be certain what business the employer was in. It appeared to be an administrative assistant role with some events coordination work.

89. Part Time Team Member

I would prefer that any member of a team I am part of, be in it for the whole shift. If you are only a 'team member' part time, then what are you for the rest of the shift? A belligerent, selfish, bludger perhaps? Hmm, this job is starting to sound appealing.

The role the employer was actually advertising:

The employer was a retail store (fashion) looking for a part-time sales assistant. Similar advertisements are seen for fast-food staff.

OFF-COLOUR OPTIONS

Some advertised job titles sound just plain wrong. Perhaps it's me and how my mind works, but I really think that advertisers should take more care to ensure that their job titles don't sound 'dodgy' or 'suspect'. If you're advertising something a little risqué, then try and make it very clear that it is the case. It'll save embarrassment on both the part of the job seeker and recruiter down the track.

This last section of the book contains some real eyebrow raisers. Enjoy!

90. Sexual Harassment Officer

Would you be interested in a busy role, involving sexually harassing and intimidating other staff? An opportunity exists for an experienced sexual harassment officer.

The role the employer was actually advertising:

A government department was looking for a base-grade officer to manage a register of sexual harassment complaints and provide information on processes and progress with investigations.

91. Lifestyle and Activities Assistant

Another vague role title that could describe anything from a physical therapist in a nursing home, to a gym instructor, to a childcare worker, to an Adult Industry worker.

The role the employer was actually advertising:

The position was advertised by a community services agency. I was unable to tell exactly what the role entailed.

92. Hand Therapy, Casual Bank

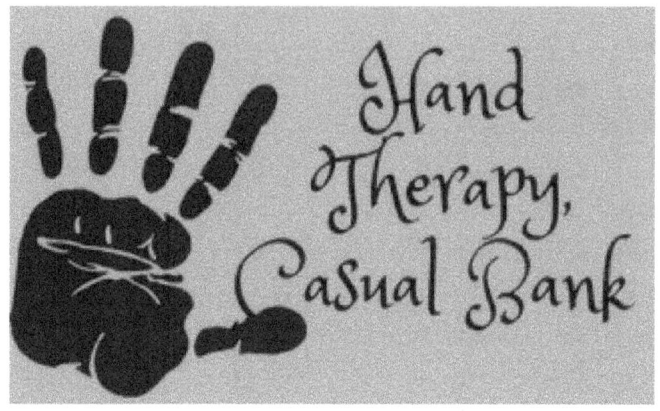

Is this position advertising for people for a casual bank? What's a casual bank? My bank is rather formal? And why would a bank need 'hand therapy'? Not sure that I want to touch this one, regardless of whether it is a full-time, part-time or casual position.

The role the employer was actually advertising:

A closer examination of the position description led me to believe that the vacancy was for casual staff members, who were qualified Occupational Therapists, specialising in hand mobility.

"You want me to do what now?"

93. Service Fulfillment Coordinator

I couldn't make out what service required fulfilling, or why they required a coordinator.

The role the employer was actually advertising:

From what I could gather, a logistics company looking for warehouse/store person to fill incoming orders placed the advertisement. Not very exciting at all.

94. Partner Relationship

Are you in a relationship? Are you looking for a relationship? Would you make a suitable partner? The job didn't specify whether the relationship was business or romantic, but it sounded rather enticing?

The role the employer was actually advertising:

No, this wasn't an advertisement placed by a dating agency looking for new members. This was an advertisement for a sales position.

95. Full Service Co-Worker

Are you looking for a 'full service'? Sounds a bit suspicious. One may assume that this is some sort of attendant for what used to be called a 'full-service garage'. For those not familiar with the concept, this is where you pull your car into the service station and someone personally comes out to the car, fills your petrol, checks the oils, and tyre pressures.

The role the employer was actually advertising:

Not actually sure what this role was describing but it certainly wasn't for petrol/gas station staff. Maybe the creepy-sounding job was actually for something risqué after all.

96. Heavy Rigid Driver

Looking for Heavy Rigid Driver, the advertisement stated. Well aren't we all ducky? Not so sure about the 'heavy' bit, but to each their own. What I love about these particular advertisements is that sometimes the words "with rear lift" is added to the end of it.

The role the employer was actually advertising:

If you are involved in the transport industry you will know what this is for straight away. The employer, most likely a trucking company, was looking for a driver who is licensed to operate heavy rigid vehicles (trucks with solid side walls).

97. Leisure Services Officer

Do you have experience offering 'leisure services'? What type of 'leisure services' is this officer required to perform? This could be for anything from an Adult Entertainment industry worker to a gym instructor.

The role the employer was actually advertising:

This employer was a local council. They were advertising for a lifeguard for a public pool.

98. Special Requests Clerk

Hmm, this sounds suspicious. What sort of 'special' requests are we talking about? If the role were to service any sort of special request then I would ask the employee for a fully paid, first-class around-the-world ticket.

The role the employer was actually advertising:

The employer was a large hotel chain, and the position advertised would normally be described as a 'Concierge'.

99. Front End Loader

I was under the impression that a 'Front End Loader" was an inanimate object - A piece of machinery used in building and construction. I'm pretty certain that they can't apply for jobs. Perhaps they want a person to be the 'Front End Loader'? Now I know that I've gained a little weight of late, but I don't think that I could pass as a piece of machinery.

The role the employer was actually advertising:

The position was actually for a suitably licensed and experienced driver and machine operator.

100. Rear Loader Driver – Waste

Oh my! This doesn't sound very attractive. What's a 'Rear Loader'? And why does it need driving?

The role the employer was actually advertising:

A bookend to the front-end loader position– In this case a local council was advertising for a garbage collector with a truck licence.

101. Members Only

> **Want to work with Members?**
>
> Positions available include:
> Member Engagement
> Member Relations
> Member Services

Okay let's end the list on a juvenile note. There are a number of different types of jobs for members. These ones have been advertised recently:

- Member Engagement Officer
- Member Relations
- Member Services

All I can say about these positions is: Oh my! All great opportunity for those who are keen on relationships with members.

The role the employer was actually advertising:

The job descriptions were very vague, but all appear to involve call centre work, specifically dealing with customer complaints. Nothing sexy here.

CLOSING REMARKS

I hope that the listings in this book have brought a smile to you face. You are of course, completely free to disagree with my assessment of the aforementioned position titles.

They are based on my opinion rather than fact. It should also be noted that some people love working in call centres, for debt collections agencies, in door-to-door sales, and in cold canvassing positions.

The job search experience can be a tough gig, and it's important to look at the lighter side of life to help get you through.

I wish you all the best in your endeavours.

ACKNOWLEDGEMENTS

With special thanks to my husband, for his on-going support and editorial prowess. My gratitude also goes out to the members of the Orchard's Apples writing group for their tireless efforts providing support, advice and proofreading at every stage of the book.

I need to say a big thank you to all of those advertisers out there, who were prepared to put out shoddy, half-baked job advertisements. I hope that you found the employees you were looking for.

INDEX

Allocations Analyst	*37*
American Restaurant/Italian Restaurant	*89*
Appointment Setter	*70*
Assistant Controlled Entity Accountant	*94*
Audience Insights Officer	*54*
Banquet Attendant	*11*
Bell Attendant	*7*
Bequest Relationship Coordinator	*63*
Brand Ambassador	*67*
Café All Rounder Lady	*30*
Capability Lead	*75*
Car Groomer	*83*
Casual Keyholder Sales Assistant	*79*
Casual Nanny	*48*
Casual Refugee Youth Worker	*45*
Client Success Specialists	*28*
Collections Customer Service	*50*
Complaints and Disputes Officer	*6*
Computer Trainer	*61*
Continuous Improvement Coordinator	*31*
Crew	*19*

Customer Service Gun	*35*
Direct Services Coordinator	*81*
Domestic Violence Advocate	*41*
Entry Level Finance	*49*
Experienced Wine Bar Attendant	*20*
Family Strengthening Officer	*58*
Farm Hand Horses	*47*
Fill Associates	*73*
First Impressions Manager	*66*
Floor Supervisor	*25*
Food and Beverage Attendant	*13*
Food and Beverage Lover	*4*
Front End Loader	*109*
Full Service Co-Worker	*105*
Grocery Stores	*86*
Ground Handler	*24*
Guest Services Agent	*72*
Gym Attendant	*15*
Gym Floor/Receptionist	*42*
Hand Therapy, Casual Bank	*102*
Heavy Rigid Driver	*106*
Help Wanted	*91*

Home Onboarding Pro	*59*
Inbound Consumer Sales	*29*
Insight Analyst	*42*
Integration Assistant	*33*
Kitchen Hand/Food Truck	*51*
Lead Generation	*34*
Leisure Services Officer	*107*
Lifestyle and Activities Assistant	*101*
Lively Animated Manager	*55*
Long Life Assistant	*10*
Loyalty Campaign Specialist	*63*
Manager Positive Behaviour Support	*64*
Management Support Officer Lead Job	*74*
Meat Team Member	*44*
Members Only	*111*
Merchandise Compliance Officer	*22*
Merchandiser Sales Support	*40*
Mission Control Centre Engagement	*57*
Opening Wine Team	*17*
Part Time Essendon	*93*
Part Time People	*82*
Part Time Team Member	*98*

Partner Relationship	*104*
Party Enthusiast	*18*
Pie Dealer	*14*
People Services Consultant	*78*
Points Person	*9*
Practice Advice Coach	*32*
Principal Consultant Rail	*46*
Product Owner/Analyst	*77*
Quality Support Advisor	*38*
Rear Loader Driver – Waste	*110*
Remote Phone Sales Executive	*39*
Replenishment Officer	*68*
Retail Artist	*21*
Sales Hunter	*27*
Service Fulfillment Coordinator	*103*
Sexual Harassment Officer	*100*
Spare Van Driver	*89*
Special Requests Clerk	*108*
Sourcing Execution Specialist	*60*
Style Consultant	*71*
Superheroes!	*53*
Talent Acquisition Specialist	*56*
The Enabling Capability Platform	*97*

The Key Worker	*92*
Therapeutic Residential Care Stand Up Staff	*80*
Third in Charge	*69*
Truck and Dog Driver	*36*
Truck Jockey	*16*
University Dockhands	*8*
Vacation Student	*12*
Vegetation Liaison Officer	*87*
Vintage Cellar Hand	*23*
Vintage Retail Assistant	*5*
Weed Programs Facilitator	*96*
Weekend Needed	*85*
Winter is Coming	*95*

ABOUT THE AUTHOR

For the first twenty years of working life, the author was employed in a variety of mostly dull government roles, with the occasionally interesting jobs in welfare, ethics, the justice system and university administration. The author has extensive experience in Human Resources Management and Recruitment.

"YOU WANT ME TO DO WHAT NOW? 101 IMPOSSIBLE SELECTION CRITERIA"

So, you've finally managed to find a job that sounds like it might be right for you. You've got a pretty good idea what the job title describes, and the title isn't one that is going to cause you any embarrassment when it appears on your business card.

What's your next step? It's time to prepare your application and answer the required selection criteria. When you look at the position description and selection criteria you discover a world of weasel words and ridiculous requests. What on earth does it all mean?

Welcome to the world of ridiculous selection criteria.

COMING SOON

www.ingramcontent.com/pod-product-compliance
Lightning Source LLC
Chambersburg PA
CBHW020912090426
42736CB00008B/600